WHY IT'S A HOLIDAY

by ANN McGOVERN

AN AUTHORS GUILD BACKINPRINT.COM EDITION

iUniverse, Inc.
Bloomington

To

LILIAN MOORE

who was born on a holiday

Why It's A Holiday

iUniverse books may be ordered through booksellers or by contacting:

iUniverse
1663 Liberty Drive
Bloomington, IN 47403
www.iuniverse.com
1-800-Authors (1-800-288-4677)

ISBN: 978-1-4502-4530-2 (sc)

Printed in the United States of America

iUniverse rev. date: 3/7/2011

Contents

New Year's Day

JANUARY 1

Tick tock. Tick tock. It is late at night. The hands on the clock move slowly, slowly, toward twelve.

Then, suddenly, there is a great noise. Whistles blow. Horns toot. Bells ring. People shout, "Happy New Year!"

It is the beginning of a bright new year. It is January 1. It is a holiday.

New Year's Day was not always on the first of January. Some people celebrated New Year's Day in March or November or April. Long ago, people called Romans celebrated the new year on March 1. They celebrated this holiday to honor the coming of spring.

The Romans did not believe in one god, as we do today. They believed in many gods. They had gods for the wind, for the sun, for the rain, for the flowers. They had gods for almost anything you can think of.

They gave these gods different names. One of them was called Janus. He was the god of beginnings and endings.

Janus had two faces. One face watched the old year go out. The other face watched the new year come in.

One day the Roman emperor said, "Janus is the god of beginnings. So why not name the beginning of the year after him? From now on, the month that begins the year will be called January."

What a party the Romans had that first New Year's
Day in January! They gave each other presents. They
drank and ate all day long. It was a time for fun—for
noisy fun.

When we blow horns and ring bells and bang on pots and pans and shout "Happy New Year!" we are doing as the Romans did thousands of years ago.

When we make promises on New Year's Day, we also do as the Romans did long ago. At that time, some Romans thought, "Janus is the god of all beginnings. So we will make new beginnings, too. We will begin the new year by promising to be better than we were last year."

We call these promises *resolutions*.

Some people say, "This year I will be more helpful"; or "This year I will stop biting my nails"; or "This year I will do what I am supposed to do right away."

In England, long, long ago, the people opened their doors at the stroke of midnight. They did this to let the old year out and the new year in.

The custom of ringing bells also began in England. Before midnight, the people covered the church bells in many layers of cloth. Ding, dong. Ding, dong. The bells rang softly.

Then, at midnight, the people snatched off the cloths. DING, DONG! DING, DONG! The church bells rang loudly, merrily, welcoming in a brand-new year.

A famous poet, Alfred Tennyson, wrote about the ringing of the bells:

Ring out the old, ring in the new,
Ring, happy bells, across the snow,
The year is going, let him go;
Ring out the false, ring in the true.

Lincoln's Birthday

FEBRUARY 12

A birthday is a special holiday. Every year, your family celebrates the day you were born. There are good wishes and gifts—maybe even a birthday cake with candles.

Your family celebrates your birthday because they love you so much.

But why do millions of people celebrate one man's birthday every February 12th?

It is because Abraham Lincoln, too, is loved.

He is still loved and remembered as one of the greatest presidents we ever had.

He was born in a little log cabin in Kentucky. He grew up in the backwoods. He grew tall and strong. He learned to cut down trees and to lift heavy logs and to work the fields.

He was still a boy when his family moved to Indiana. When he was about eleven years old a school was built nine miles away from his home. The long distance didn't bother Abe. He wanted to go to school more than anything.

"Nonsense," his father said. "What does a boy want with reading and writing and 'rithmetic when he can plow a field and chop down a tree?"

But Abe *wanted* to go to that school.

And that winter he did. He walked nine miles through wind and snow and bitter cold. After school, he walked nine miles home again.

At night, his father watched the boy who stayed up so late reading by the light of the fire.

"What are you going to *do* with your learning, Abe?" he asked.

"I'm going to be President," Abe answered.

Spring came and the fields were ready for plowing. Abe's father needed help. So Abe had to leave school. But that did not stop him from studying. Everywhere he went he carried a book. He read in the fields while his horses were resting.

And every night he read by firelight. He had no pencil to write with, so he used a piece of burned wood. He had no paper to write on, so he used a wooden shovel.

People for miles around knew how hard Abe worked to learn. They knew other things about Abe, too. They knew he was kind and helpful and honest. They loved to hear his funny stories and jokes.

When he was grown, he left home to make his own way in the world. Wherever he went he made friends.

He never stopped reading. Now he read books about government and law. He became a lawyer. Later he became a member of Congress.

This was a time when our country was in great trouble. The people in the North and the people in the South had many arguments.

Should new states be allowed to have slaves?

"No!" said the people in the North. "No man should be owned by another. This is a free country."

"Yes!" said the people in the South. "We need slaves to help us grow cotton and tobacco."

Lincoln hated the idea of slavery. In Congress he repeated the words that were written when our country was new: "All men are created equal."

Lincoln loved peace. He tried to stop a war between the states. But soon after he was elected President in 1860, the Civil War began.

The men in the North and the men in the South fought each other. Many were killed.

While the terrible war was going on, Lincoln made a speech on the battleground of Gettysburg, Pennsylvania. At the end of his speech, he spoke of his hopes for his country: ". . . that this nation under God shall have a new birth of freedom, and that government of the people, by the people, and for the people shall not perish from the earth."

While the terrible war was going on, Lincoln said that all men who were slaves should be free.

Abraham Lincoln was elected President for the second time in 1864. A short time after that, the South surrendered.

Now Lincoln worked harder than ever to make the North and the South friends.

One night he went to a theater to see a play. A man crept up behind him. He held a gun in his hand. The man fired. Lincoln fell forward. The next morning he was dead.

But the memory of the things he said and the things he did will never die. Abraham Lincoln was one of the greatest men our country has ever known.

And that is why we celebrate his birthday every February 12th.

Washington's Birthday

FEBRUARY 22

February is a month of special birthdays.

Abraham Lincoln was born on February 12. And the first President of the United States was born on February 22.

George Washington was born on a big farm in

the year 1732 in the state of Virginia.

When he was a young boy, he loved adventure. He played soldier with his friends and made himself the captain.

When he grew older, he still loved adventure.

"I shall go to sea and be a sailor," he said.

But his mother said, "No! The life of a seaman is filled with danger. Some of the captains are cruel and will treat you worse than a dog."

George was not yet a man when he got his first job. That job was to mark out miles of land to show how much land a man owned. Now George did not feel so bad about not going to sea.

"There is adventure in the wilderness, too," he thought. "There is as much adventure in the wild lands as there is on the wild sea."

He came to know the wilderness better than anyone else. And he fought against the French and Indians.

In the days of George Washington, our country was divided into thirteen colonies which were owned

by England. The people were not happy being ruled by the king of England.

The day came when they wanted to be free. They wanted to be free so much they were willing to fight for their freedom.

Now George Washington had fought in wars before. He knew the ways of fighting as well as he knew the ways of the wilderness.

He was the right man to lead soldiers. He was made a general.

For six years he bravely led the soldiers into battle against England. His job was very hard. His army had not been trained to fight. They were young boys, farmers, shopkeepers.

There were never enough men, clothes, guns, or enough food.

But General Washington led his men to victory. At last the war was won. The soldiers went back to their homes. And Washington went back to his home in Mt. Vernon, Virginia.

But our country still needed a leader.

So George Washington became the first President of the United States.

That is why he is known as the Father of our Country.

And that is why we celebrate his birthday every year on February 22.

For George Washington was "first in war, first in peace, and first in the hearts of his countrymen."

Memorial Day MAY 30

Many years before the two world wars, there was another terrible war. This was the Civil War or, as it is sometimes called, the War Between the States.

Abraham Lincoln was President when that war was fought. The soldiers of the North fought the soldiers of the South.

When the war was over, a special day was set aside to honor the soldiers who had given their lives in battle. This special day was called Decoration Day. Flowers were placed on the graves of the soldiers of the North and the soldiers of the South.

Not many years ago the name of Decoration Day was changed to Memorial Day. In most states, it is celebrated on May 30th.

Independence Day

JULY 4

The Fourth of July is a big birthday. It is the birthday of our country.

Once there was no United States of America. Once our country was divided into thirteen little parts, called colonies.

Our colonies were not free. They were owned by England. The King of England made the rules. Some of them were not fair. But they had to be obeyed, whether the colonies liked them or not. For the people were not free to make up their own rules.

The rules became harder and harder to obey. Many people wanted to break away from England. They wanted to be free!

Then great men from the thirteen colonies met together in Philadelphia in June, 1776. They wrote down why they wanted to be free. They wrote down why England was not fair.

For a whole month the great men worked. They went over every word that was written down.

Then, on the fourth day of July, they said, "This paper says what we want it to say. This paper says we want to be free!"

Outside the building crowds of people gathered.

"Will the men sign the paper?" they said.

"Will they all agree to all the words they have written?"

The people were hot and uncomfortable standing there in the hot July sun.

But still they waited. Their eyes were on the door and on the big bell above the building.

Suddenly the door opened. A boy ran out into the street. His eyes were shining with excitement. Waving his arms, he shouted to the bell-man.

"Ring! Ring! RING!" The bell rang loud and clear.

It rang all day. It rang for freedom.

It told the people that our country had declared itself free. It told the country that the great men had signed their paper—the Declaration of Independence.

On the Fourth of July, 1776, our country was born.

And every year we celebrate that birthday.

Labor Day

Once a year, Americans celebrate work. They celebrate work by not working at all!

This holiday is called Labor Day.

A carpenter by the name of Peter Maguire thought of Labor Day less than a hundred years ago.

It was his idea to set aside a day to honor all the people who work. It was his idea that the first Monday in September should be named Labor Day.

The first Labor Day was celebrated in 1882.

Offices and factories were closed.

Banks were closed.

The stores were closed.

There was a big parade in New York City.

Hundreds of workingmen marched in the parade.

From state to state the idea of celebrating Labor Day spread.

Today, working men and women in every state celebrate the day that honors them!

Columbus Day

OCTOBER 12

Long, long ago there lived a small boy who loved the sea more than anything else.

He loved the smell of the salty sea.

He loved to watch the ships come and go.

"Someday I will sail across the sea," he thought.

"I will sail across the sea to new lands."

What big dreams for such a little boy!

"Christopher Columbus!" his mother scolded. "You are a weaver's son. But do you weave cloth? Oh, no! You weave dreams. Dreams of the sea, that's what you weave!"

In the days of Columbus, almost 500 years ago, people did not know as much about the world as they do today. Many people thought that the world was flat, shaped like a saucer or a pancake.

They said, "If a ship sailed to the edge of the world, it would fall off the edge and be lost forever."

They spoke of oceans that boiled hot, and sea dragons waiting to eat sailors who sailed too far.

But Columbus studied about the world and about the sea. He studied maps and charts. He felt sure that the world was round, like a ball or an apple. He learned all about sailing and all about ships. He planned to sail west across the sea someday.

"If I sail west across the sea, I will get to India," he thought. "India—the land filled with rich treasures."

But no one would believe him. No one would listen to his plan or give him money for his voyage.

Years went by. At last the King and Queen of Spain listened to his plan. They did not make fun of his dream. They gave him money for his voyage.

And so, in 1492, Columbus set sail from Spain. More than a hundred men sailed with him. Over an unknown sea they sailed west on three little wooden ships—the *Nina*, the *Pinta*, and the *Santa Maria*.

For days they sailed.

For weeks they sailed.

The sailors were frightened. Never before had they sailed so long without seeing land.

"Turn back!" they begged Columbus. "Turn back before the sea dragons eat us!"

But Christopher Columbus said, "Sail on! Sail on to India!"

He was not afraid.

He knew there were no sea dragons.

At last the frightened sailors said, "TURN BACK! Or we will throw you overboard!"

Columbus thought and thought. He said to himself, "Land is near. I know it. I feel it. But how can I make my sailors believe it?"

Then, from out of the sky, came hope. A flock of birds flew overhead. Branches floated by. These were sure signs that land was near.

Now there was no more talk of turning back. Now the sailors watched for the first sight of land.

And just before the dawn of October 12, 1492, came a cry from the *Pinta*.

"Land! Land ahead!"

Christopher Columbus saw a sandy beach shining in the moonlight. He saw palm trees swaying in the breeze.

"India!" he cried as he planted the flag of Spain into the soil of the new land. "At last I have reached India. I will call the people of this land *Indians*."

Back to Spain he sailed. Back to the King and Queen who had given him the money for the voyage.

In Spain Columbus was called a hero for reaching India.

But the people did not know, nor did Columbus, that he had *not* reached India. He had reached another land instead.

And that land is our America.

Christopher Columbus had discovered America, and in doing so had proved that the world is round.

And so we celebrate October 12 as Columbus Day, the day Christopher Columbus landed in America.

Election Day

Men and women in the United States are lucky. They can choose the people they want as leaders of their city, state, and country. They do this by voting for them.

The people in some countries cannot do this.

In the United States, men and women choose their leaders on Election Day. Millions of Americans line up and wait for their turn to vote. They line up at

schools and churches, at firehouses and stores. These places are turned into voting places on Election Day.

Sometimes the voters vote on new laws, as well as for the men and women they think can do the best job. Sometimes they vote whether to build a new road, or playground. They vote on many important matters.

Every four years, our country elects its President on Election Day. This day comes on the first Tuesday after the first Monday in November.

Some people vote by marking a paper. Other people vote on special voting machines. Everyone's vote is a secret. No one has to tell whom he voted for.

Through the years, men have worked hard to give everyone the right to vote.

When our country was young, men who did not own their own homes could not vote. And until 1920 women were not allowed to vote. Now almost everyone who is twenty-one years old can vote.

The votes of people help to keep America free. So Election Day is a very important day.

Veterans Day

NOVEMBER 11

In 1914 a terrible war began. Many countries fought in that war, including the United States.

This war was called a World War because men from countries all over the world were fighting in it.

For four years cannons roared. Men in planes fought each other in the skies.

At last came the day when the cannons were silent, when the planes did not go up.

It was November 11, 1918.

Soldiers everywhere laid down their guns. There was no more fighting.

The warring countries had agreed to end the war. This agreement was called an armistice. And the day on which it was signed became known as Armistice Day.

News of the armistice spread quickly. In every big city, in every tiny town, there was a big celebration.

People ran into the streets shouting the wonderful news.

PEACE!

Everybody was happy that the World War was over. But they were sad, too. They thought of the soldiers who would never come home. They thought of the men who had died for their country.

The armistice was signed on the eleventh hour of the eleventh day of the eleventh month of the year.

And so every year, at eleven o'clock in the morning

of November 11th, people all over the United States stop working or playing. They stop to think of the brave men who fought for peace.

After that first World War, the people hoped and dreamed that there would never be another war. But that dream did not come true. For there was a second World War, even more terrible than the first. And after that war was over, there was still another war —the Korean War.

In 1954, President Eisenhower changed the name of this special day from Armistice Day to Veterans Day. On November 11 we honor the men and women who fought for our country—the war veterans.

Thanksgiving

The sky was gray and the sea was rough. The little ship tossed about on the stormy sea.

On the *Mayflower* one hundred and two passengers crowded together. The rocking of the ship made some of the passengers seasick. Others were sick because there were not enough fresh fruits and vegetables to eat.

The governor of Plymouth called the Pilgrims together and made a brief speech.

"We have much to be thankful for," he said. "Let us set aside a special day to thank God for this good harvest."

The day was set. The Indians were invited.

From the forests, the men brought back deer and turkey. From the streams and from the sea they brought back fish and eels and clams.

The women cooked and cooked. They baked pies and made bread. They cleaned and polished and scrubbed.

The special day arrived. The Indians came with a present of five deer.

So much company!

So much food!

Chief Massasoit and ninety Indians sat down to the first Thanksgiving dinner in America.

The Pilgrims said prayers of Thanksgiving. They thanked God for the good harvest, their comfortable homes, their warm clothes. They thanked God for their new friends who taught them the new ways of a new land. And they thanked God for the country where they were free to go to their own church.

The sun went down. But the Indians stayed. They stayed for three days. They played games and sang songs. And they ate and ate and ate.

That first Thanksgiving dinner took place more than 300 years ago.

And every year, on the fourth Thursday of November, Americans give thanks for the food on the table, for family and for friends, and for their country and their freedom.

They give thanks, just as the Pilgrims did long, long, ago.

Christmas DECEMBER 25

Christmas means something special all over the world.

Christmas means a Christmas tree with glass balls, shining silver, and bright lights. It means Christmas songs and Christmas carols. It means Christmas greens, holly and ivy. It means Santa Claus.

Christmas means the Christmas story. The story of the birthday of the Christ Child.

Christmas means a special hope. The hope that there will be PEACE ON EARTH and GOOD WILL TOWARD MEN.

Christmas begins with a birthday. This is the story the Bible tells us. The Emperor of Rome wanted to count all the people. For this count, each man had to go back to the town he came from. A carpenter called Joseph and his wife Mary went to Bethlehem. The town was crowded. There was no place for Mary and Joseph to stay. There was no room at the inn. But there *was* room in the stable. So they stayed in the stable with all the farm animals.

The time had come for Mary to have her child. And that night, in the stable, Jesus was born.

Near by, shepherds were watching their sheep in the field. Suddenly they saw a shining light. The light seemed to shine everywhere. The shepherds were frightened. Then, from out of the light, an angel appeared. The angel said, "Fear not. I bring you good tidings of great joy. For unto you is born this day Christ the Lord."

The shepherds went to the inn. There in the stable they saw the infant Jesus lying in the manger.

That night a bright star shone over Bethlehem. Three Wise Men from far away saw the star. To Bethlehem they came, bringing rich gifts for the new-born Christ Child.

This is the story that is told each Christmas.

Sometimes the story is told in songs.

Singing Christmas carols began hundreds of years ago in England. The men in England went from house to house singing their songs. We still hear some of these same songs.

Oh what fun to give presents and to get presents on Christmas morning! Some say this idea started when Jesus was born, and the Three Wise Men came to Bethlehem to bring Him their gifts.

The Three Wise Men did not place their gifts under a Christmas tree. The idea of Christmas trees did not begin until much later.

It is said that Martin Luther, a famous man in Germany, took a walk on Christmas Eve. He saw the stars shining in the sky. He saw the snow on the dark ground.

"How beautiful this holy night is," he thought. He wanted to share his good thoughts. So he cut down a small fir tree and brought it inside for his wife and children to see.

Why do we decorate our houses with ivy and holly and other green branches? Some say this idea began in Germany thousands of years ago. At that time the people believed that good spirits lived in holly trees.

"We will bring the holly inside," they said. "The good spirits of the Wood will bring us luck."

Although no one has ever seen him, every girl and boy has heard of Santa Claus.

The little children in Holland were the first to know about Santa, long, long ago. In Holland he is called St. Nicholas. In other lands he is called Kris Kringle or Father Christmas.

Christmas is the best holiday of the year. For it means something special all over the world.

SPECIAL
RELIGIOUS
HOLIDAYS

Easter and Good Friday

Easter week brings days of sadness and days of gladness. To many people, Good Friday is the saddest day of the year. It was on a Friday, almost two thousand years ago, that Jesus Christ died on the cross. In many churches, the services on Good Friday last for three hours.

Two days after Good Friday comes Easter Sunday. Easter comes on a different date each year. But whenever it comes —in March or in April—it is a joyful day.

Easter eggs.

Easter rabbits.

New spring clothes.

The Easter story.

That's what Easter is.

The Bible tells us the Easter story. Two days after Jesus died, some friends came to visit his grave early Sunday morning. But the grave was empty!

How frightened the friends were! Just then an angel came and sat down on the empty grave.

"He is not here," the angel said. "For He is risen."

Then the friends were filled with joy.

"Christ is risen!" they said.

Ever since then, Easter Sunday has been a joyful day. A day to celebrate the great miracle when Jesus rose from the dead to live forever in Heaven.

To many people, Easter means the coming of spring.

Thousands of years ago, before Easter became a holiday, many people celebrated the coming of spring. They had a goddess of spring called Eostre. In the spring, the people held a merry party in her honor. The name Easter comes from the goddess Eostre.

Have you ever wondered what rabbits and eggs have to do with Easter?

Eggs stand for the beginning of a new life. To celebrate this new life, people gave each other presents of eggs. They made the eggs look as bright and as gay as the earth looks in springtime. They colored the eggs with bright colors.

And long ago, people believed rabbits stood for new life. In those days, mothers told their little children stories of the Easter rabbit.

"On the night before Easter, the Easter rabbit is very busy," mothers used to say. "He hops here and he hops there. Everywhere he hops he lays colored eggs in the new spring grass."

Easter is also the day for dressing up in new spring clothes. People have been doing this for hundreds of years. Today, grownups and children take part in a special parade. All you have to do to join the Easter Parade in your town is to dress up in your new spring clothes and take a walk on Easter Sunday.

Rosh Hashanah

Rosh Hashanah is the Jewish New Year. Rosh Hashanah means "the beginning of the year." On this day, the Jews believe, God opens a big Book of Life in heaven. In the book God sees what everyone has done, said, or thought all year, and He writes down, the names of those who deserve to have a good new year.

When Jews meet one another, they say "May you be inscribed for a good year!" That means they hope God has decided to give them a happy new year.

In the temple, a ram's horn blows. The services begin. The people pray that God will forgive their mistakes.

Yom Kippur

The most serious Jewish holiday is the Day of Atonement, ten days after Rosh Hashanah. This day is called Yom Kippur. Many Jews over thirteen years old will go without food all day. They will pray in the temple all day—until they hear the long note of the ram's horn.

Then they know that the Book of Life is closed until the next year.

Succoth

Five days after Yom Kippur comes Succoth. This happy holiday lasts nine days.

The Jews left Egypt, the Bible tells us, and wandered in the desert for forty years. Before the Jews reached the Promised Land, they lived in shelters made from dry branches. Today Jewish families make their own little outdoor shelters to honor the Jews of long ago. They decorate them with flowers, fruit, and branches. They even eat their meals in the little leafy houses.

Since Succoth comes in the fall, Jews thank God for their good harvest. So Succoth is the Jewish Thanksgiving, too.

Hanukkah

Hanukkah is known as the Feast of Lights. This happy eight-day holiday comes in the wintertime. It is a time for presents and parties. Young children play with small, four-sided tops. On each side of the top is a Hebrew letter which stands for these words: *A great miracle happened there.*

Jewish children hear the story of the great miracle. A foreign king and his army took over Palestine and the big temple there. For three years, the Jews fought their enemy. At last the Jews won the fight. They won back their city and their temple.

Inside the temple a light was always kept burning. The Jews looked for oil to light their holy lamps. But they found only enough oil to last one day. Then the great miracle happened! The light burned for eight days and eight nights. That gave the Jews enough time to prepare more oil.

Ever since then, Jews around the world celebrate Hanukkah. They light candles in a special candlestick called the *Menorah*. There is a candle for each of the eight days the light burned in the temple long ago. On the first night of Hanukkah, the first candle is lit. Every night, another candle is added until all eight candles burn on the last night of this winter holiday.

Passover

Long ago, an Egyptian king made all the Jews slaves. For 430 years, the Jews were owned by cruel masters until Moses led them to freedom. Moses and the Jews left Egypt in such a hurry that they had no time to make proper bread. They mixed together flour and water, but without yeast the bread did not rise. So they ate the flat or *unleavened* bread.

Today, when the Jews celebrate Passover every spring, they eat the same kind of bread. They call this bread *matzoth*.

Passover lasts eight days. It begins with a big dinner called the *Seder*. On the table there are special foods. Some foods remind the Jews of the terrible days when their people were slaves. Other foods remind them of the happy days when their people became free.

OTHER SPECIAL DAYS

Arbor Day

Almost a hundred years ago, a man named J. Sterling Morton looked at the land of Nebraska. "The land is bare and the soil is dry. This land needs trees to hold the soil in place and to make the land beautiful." He thought there should be a special day for planting trees. He called this day Arbor Day. In 1872, more than a million trees were planted in Nebraska. The trees grew tall and straight. To-day, every state in the country celebrates Arbor Day, the tree-planting day.

Valentine's Day

FEBRUARY 14

Thousands of years ago wild wolves roamed Europe. The Romans thought a special god would protect them from the wolves. So they gave a party in the god's honor every February. And they noticed that on the day of the party the birds seemed to choose their mates. "We will do the same," the Romans said. So men gave gifts to their sweethearts and wrote them love letters. Years later a special name was given to this holiday to honor two saints named Valentine.

April Fool's Day

APRIL 1

Long ago, New Year's Day came on April 1 instead of January 1. Then a new calendar was made. January 1 became New Year's Day. But some people did not like to change

their old holiday. On April 1, they greeted their friends saying, "Happy New Year!" Some of their friends said, "New Year's Day is January 1. This is April! You are an April fool!" And little by little, the first of April became a day for fooling and for being fooled.

Flag Day

JUNE 14

The first American flag had seven red and six white stripes with thirteen white stars upon a blue background. This became our official flag on June 14, 1777. Every year, on that day, we honor our flag's birthday. It waves over our free land. Our flag still has thirteen stripes which stand for our first states. But our flag now has fifty stars—one for each state in the nation.

United Nations Day

OCTOBER 24

A big world war was over. From all over the world people came to a meeting in California. "Let's have no more war," they said. "Let's work together to settle our fights." They formed the United Nations. They wrote the United Nations Charter. On October 24, 1945, fifty-one nations signed the Charter and agreed to follow its rules. Since then, more than thirty other countries have joined the United Nations. They work hard so that all countries in the world can live as good neighbors.

Halloween

OCTOBER 31

Thousands of years ago, in England, Halloween was a night of terror. No one dressed up and *pretended* to be ghosts and witches. Everyone *believed* there really were such things. "Fire will keep them away," they said. So they lit huge fires on the hills. They cut holes in turnips and placed candles inside. So when you light your jack-o'-lanterns and dress up in scary costumes, you are following customs that are thousands of years old.

A note to the readers:

Why It's A Holiday was first published in 1960, before there were other holidays to celebrate. Today we celebrate Martin Luther King Day, Earth Day, Kwanza and others.

You can look up these holidays on the computer or in your library. And my new web site will be finished in June of 2011. Go to www.annmcgovern.com, then click on Why It's A Holiday and go to the More Holidays link.

I hope you enjoyed this book. It was my first book! Since then, I wrote over 40 more!